How to Be
A BIG SISTER

A Warm Story to Prepare for a New Baby Sibling

This story, adapted from children's retellings by a team of inspired parents and teachers, aims to help your child feel positive about welcoming a new baby.

MamTalk
BOOKS FOR KIDS

A Gift for

....

From

....

Date

....

Once upon a time, I lived happily with my Mom and Dad.

I loved to blow bubbles that floated up high, jump rope, and play with a balloon! But playing alone wasn't much fun.

One day, I told my Mom and Dad,
"I wish I had a brother or sister!
It's more fun to play together!"
Yay! My parents agreed! I was so happy! By the
way, they don't always give me what I ask for!
Want to know what happened next? Then listen!

Unfortunately, my new brother or sister didn't come right away. First, the baby grew in Mom's tummy. Her tummy got bigger every day.

Dad and I took care of Mom a lot.

Finally, the big day came! Dad took Mom to the hospital. Don't worry! Mom is okay! She just needs the doctors' help to bring the baby into the world.

Mom said I had to stay home with my nanny. I agreed because I wanted the baby to be born safely.

We got ready for the baby. We required a crib, a baby table, bottles, a baby bathtub, and so much more!

Finally, we went to the hospital to bring Mom and the baby home! We brought chocolates and flowers for Mom and a beautiful stroller for the baby.

Mom hugged me and said, "I can't believe you're so grown up. You're a big sister now! I still remember the day we brought you home for the first time."

The baby is so tiny and wrinkly. I realize the baby can't play with me yet. But I know my lovely new baby sibling will grow up soon.

The baby cries a lot because newborn babies can't talk. Mom has to take care of the baby a lot and I understand I need to help my Mom. After all, I am a big sister now.

I can help my Mom change the baby's diapers, hold the bottle, bring the pacifier, rock the baby's crib, sing a song for the baby, and walk together in the park.

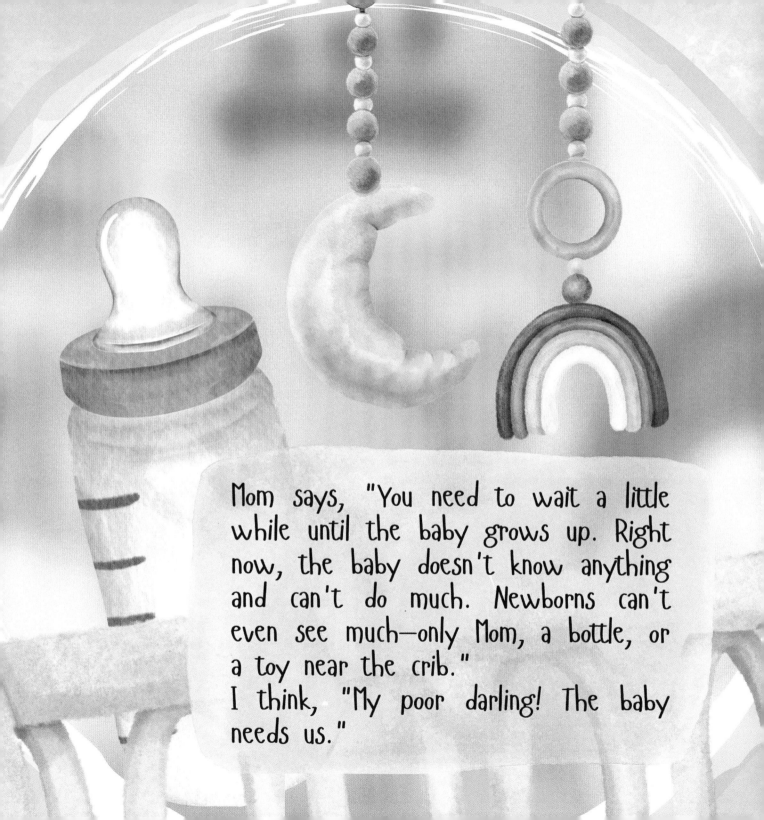

Mom says, "You need to wait a little while until the baby grows up. Right now, the baby doesn't know anything and can't do much. Newborns can't even see much—only Mom, a bottle, or a toy near the crib."

I think, "My poor darling! The baby needs us."

Mom is right. The baby needs our help. The baby doesn't know anything about our world. The baby was swimming in Mom's tummy and suddenly arrived here. We need to help the baby feel at home!

Don't be afraid, baby!
I'll show you our house, the yard, the street, and the park!
Don't worry, baby!
I'll wait for you to grow up!
And then we will play together!

You are the best sister in the world!

This story is **adapted from kids' retellings** by a team of **inspired parents and teachers** to help your little girl **feel positive about welcoming a new baby.**

We love helping parents and kids. **Your review will help us become even more helpful to our readers.** Thank you for choosing us!

Simply **find the book** and **review section here:**

AMAZON.COM/DP/B0D4CW9LYF